S.T.R.I.P.

A Stripper's 20 Life Winning Lessons

Essence Revealed
Creator of the 5 Day Fearless Challenge & the 6-
Week S.T.R.I.P. Shift program

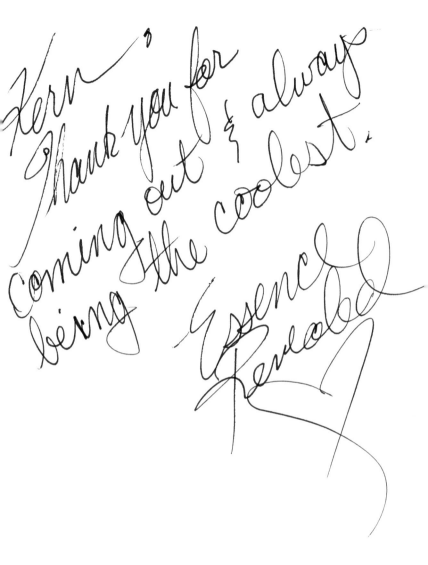

Kern,
Thank you for
coming out & always
being the coolest.

Essence
Revealed

Table of Contents

PREFACE

I didn't become a stripper to pay for college.

In fact, I had already been to college...twice. I had been lied to my whole life. A college education was not the only "key" to success. Yes, I needed an education, but it didn't need to be in the form of a fancy, overpriced, framed degree. Two degrees later, I finally got my "real" education through stripping.

I became a stripper to support my passion for performing. I worked in strip clubs in New York, New Jersey, and Las Vegas for about a decade in hiding. I had a deep fear of the stigma attached to being a stripper. I feared that I'd no longer be taken seriously as an intelligent human being because I danced topless for a living. I even feared that I was locking myself out of future opportunities as an actor, despite knowing the flexibility that stripping provided. I was able to make enough money to be able to attend auditions.

But do you know what my biggest fear was? Getting to the end of my life never pursuing acting, never giving my all to my passion for film and the stage. If stripping could help me get there, maybe even giving me an additional training ground, I had to at least try it.

I needed a way to cover my living expenses, college loan payments, and all the costs for a creative life. It doesn't matter if you're a full-time actor or another type of artist, there are costs for supplies, classes, networking, and tools of the trade, such as pictures, business cards, clothing, and more. Art schools teach very little about the business of being an artist. Anyone who has pursued show business has to quickly learn how to run a business, not just be a creative. When you get into the real arts world, outside of university/conservatory training, you learn that it's so much more than showing the skills of a deeply studied craft. There are many talented people who will never make a living from their art because of missing links, such as who you know, who you're related to, who you're dating, timing, opportunity, an advocate in the business, and just sheer luck. Yes, luck.

Funny enough, learned skills from being an actor are what helped me (along with therapy) to exit the strip club business as mentally and spiritually intact as possible. No one escapes unchanged, but I was able to create a stripper persona, who was not truly "me." While stripping funded my acting career, my acting skills helped me navigate stripper life. My stripper persona is still a character I lean on, even outside of the strip club. She's confident, unfazed and present in the moment. Anything said to her easily rolls off, insults and compliments alike. She's the opposite of my naturally introverted, socially awkward, homebody self.

I entered the strip club to earn money and exited with an education on living a life that is super valuable to me. This education helped me master many jobs I've had during and after my time working in strip clubs. I've worked as a licensed realtor, art model, bartender, executive assistant, teaching artist, instructor, an internationally crowned, traveling burlesque performer and now as a self actualization strategist for survivors of sexual violence.

As women, we are socialized to create a tug of war between our true selves and a self that we think is more "acceptable" or makes other people comfortable.

I am on a continuous journey to live life as authentically, real, and open as possible. I will not hide in a world that wants me to smother who I am (especially the sexy parts). I own that I am simultaneously an intelligent and sexual being and I'm often asked two questions: 1. What *really* goes on in a strip club? 2. How have you been able to be bold about putting yourself out there and freelance for twenty years? In *S.T.R.I.P. - A Stripper's 20 Life Winning Lessons*, I share twenty powerful ways my stripper education taught me how to win in real life through my unexpected education in the club.

21-Day Challenge:

To integrate and put into practice the lessons learned in *S.T.R.I.P. - A Stripper's 20 Life Winning Lessons*, I recommend a twenty-day challenge to experience ways in which you can bring some of the lessons in the book into your real life.

They say it takes 21-days to form a habit. So, let's do that time and focus on good things. What we focus on expands. I believe our thoughts are prayers to the universe. Therefore, worry is a prayer for something we don't want. For the next 20 days, we're going to work with some of the lessons in this book and journal what happens.

We live in a time where we are bombarded with news and information 24-7, which can create a view that is focused on fear and impending doom. A feel-good story is a special report not the norm. Let's seek the inverse.

To this end, let's start each day with at least 30-minutes of Social Media Free time. No Facebook, Instagram, Twitter, Snapchat, Pinterest, nothing but spending time with you: read, meditate, dance, exercise, listen to some 'get pumped up' or soothing jams, write, or do absolutely nothing. But NO SOCIAL MEDIA as soon as our eyes pop open in the morning.

Every few chapters there will be an exercise to work on during the week. The goal is to get you thinking about things in a different way. It is about challenging yourself from the inside out so that you proceed in life working that way - from the inside out versus from the outside in. What we think, feel, and desire should be the signal we use to proceed or not in life. Replace thoughts about outside judgement, critique or disapproval with an honest assessment of what you want to manifest, and what feels good to you. Let's get your mindset focused on possibilities instead of limiting fear. Let's get your mindset tuned into you and away from fears about outside feedback.

21-Day Challenge

Week 1 (Day 1 - 5):

Go through the next five days this week taking note of good the things that both happen to you and you witness happen to others. At the end of the day, write down five good things that happened during the day.

Bonus: Save a dollar each day this week.

1) REJECTION HAS NO POWER

OVER ME

"Most fears of rejection rest on the desire for approval from other people. Don't base your self-esteem on their opinions." - **Harvey Mackay**

I'm an introvert. I am a homebody. I love books more than socializing with strangers. Stripping required me to be social with a large number of strangers every single night. So obviously, you can see where that was going to be a problem for me. But I knew that if I was going to make any money at stripping, I had to get over being an introvert, the discomfort of asking for money, and my fear of rejection.

As a stripper, I heard countless no's night after night, week after week, year after year. The result was I was trained to feel "no" with way less impact. I had to, if I was going to survive in this line of work. While not getting an acting role can be disappointing, it's still an easier form of rejection, as the judgement is based on a specific role you've played, not you being personally rejected. Acting rejections are also a silent no; you only hear back from the casting director if you are in the final choices or you got the part.

Now, hearing "no" as a stripper….that's an entirely different experience.

Hearing "no" in a strip club is harsh. It's face-to-face rejection. People don't feel the need to be polite to strippers. "No" can come in the form of a gentle brush off, an "I'm not into (insert your type here)," and endless numbers of "come back later" or even ugly insults. I once had a group of foreign businessmen hold their hands straight out in front of them and twist their faces in utter disgust, furiously waving their hands, "NO!"

Being rejected can shake your confidence, if you let it. I've heard "no" all day as an actor, then I heard "no" as a stripper for most of the night. People imagine stripping as an easy job where you waltz in and a few hours later you magically have thousands of dollars. Here's the truth...it is hours of searching for someone who will say "yes." Just like in "regular" life, strippers hear "no" way more than they hear "yes" too. It would have been debilitating in all of my careers if

I gave rejection *any* power over me. So, I simply posed these questions to myself.

What if I took away "no's" power?

What if "no" had zero charge over me?

But then most important question came to mind…

"How the heck can hearing rejection not a big deal?"

It starts by reframing "no" in our minds. The same way I didn't take not getting an acting part as personal rejection, was the same way I was able to not take "no's" in the strip clubs personally either. It really is okay that not everyone wants to work with you, date you, buy from you, book you or get a dance from you. This is just a simple fact of life. Everyone won't be your client or customer (yes, even if they are your friend).

I chose to get into the flow of "no's" by taking more risks and searching for opportunities to hear "no" more. The truth is the more swings you take at the bat, the more you'll miss, BUT also, the more likely you're to hit home runs and hear "YES!"

I learned as a stripper that every "no" is a pathway to a great "yes." By "traditional beauty standards," I'd watch women who were rated 10's or 11's make way less money than women considered "less attractive." These "pretty girls" would talk among themselves about their disbelief in how a "regular" looking woman was making more money than them. "How?!" They were in utter shock and disbelief. But while they were stumped, I was taking notes.

While they were standing in a pretty woman bunch insulting plain jane, plain jane was on the floor talking to everyone, taking way more swings with the bat. Plain jane was out there asking for the sale. She heard way more no's than the pretty woman bunch, but that also meant she heard way more yeses too.

Many of the pretty women preferred for men to approach them. Many would change dresses or take a break after every "no." I would hear some ladies talk about how "this dress" isn't making them any money. Or complaints that the customers were cheap that tonight. In actuality, waiting to be picked instead of initiating a conversation was what wasn't making her any money. She thought being beautiful and standing there should be enough. Or she allowed fear to stop her from approaching customers. The floor of a strip club is not like being on the street outside. There are many beautiful women in a club. Sorry, pretty lady, you have to initiate conversations with many people to make money in a strip club!

I realized that I needed to collect more no's in my endeavors as that was the quickest way to get to more yes's. I reframed "no" in my mind and realized that I couldn't lose what I didn't have in the first place. So, what does "no" take away from me? Absolutely nothing. But not going for the opportunity, the ask, the risk...that could potentially take away a "yes." I know I'm doing my job when I hear "no."

One day, I stumbled into attempting to collect a "no." I was running the sound booth for a voice over class taught by an agent. I convinced myself at some point after the class began, that he was enamored with the blonde with the gravelly voice in the class. As far as I was concerned, I was just getting a free class. Once there was a natural pause, I raised my hand and announced that I needed to go to the bathroom. He wasn't going to be working with me so why bust my bladder being over accommodating?

At the very end of class, he gave me his card. I figured it was because I had recorded everyone. I was kind of an an employee in the class. I asked, "Are you going to act like you don't know who I am when I call tomorrow? Because unlike most people, I actually do follow up." He assured me he would remember me. I'd been working with him for twenty-four years and three agencies later. I figured he would have told me no at that point, so I just relaxed and decided to be my real self versus my perky easy to work with actor self. What if I hadn't asked? What if I hadn't relaxed?

Are there times when you think you're being polite but really, it's just fear of rejection? Manners do count and being outlandish is never going to work favorably either. Can you think of a situation where you experienced fear like this in your past? If yes, awesome! Do not beat yourself up over it. Right now decide what you will do when an opportunity like this arises again. If when I get an opportunity to XYZ, then I will *do* XYZ. Meditate on that every once in a while to keep it top of mind. A mantra like this isn't about whether you believe it or not. It's about a promise to yourself to take a specific action. No belief. Just action. What do you commit to? What steps will you actively take to reach your desired destination? Are you willing to schedule it and breathe through any fear that convinces you to break your promise to yourself? There are things in life that are worth facing, the seemingly insurmountable challenge for. What is that thing in your life?

"There is going to be a hundred thousand doors slammed in your face before one opens, so feel ok about taking rejection." - **Heather Matarazzo**

2) APPROACH AS IF YOU'VE

ALREADY WON

"Expect everything to happen for your benefit yet do not insist on how it must be experienced. Allow yourselves to be surprised. Remember that what you expect with your physical mind is the least you can be offered by your all-knowing-Self." - **Raphael Zernoff**

When I first started dancing, I'd approach men in a friendly but timid way. I'd hope and wish for a "yes," but surely didn't expect to hear it. Sometimes, I'd get a "yes," sometimes I'd get a "no." I'd watch dancers with more experience than I had get "yes's" all the time. And for the life of me, I couldn't figure out what I was doing wrong.

I'd be looking good, smelling good, feeling good. Like seriously...what was the issue? It was simple actually. The issue was that I didn't expect a "yes." "Yes" was a pleasant surprise, not an expected outcome. Therefore, I came off uncertain and weak when I approached customers.

Think about it…

How much trust would you put in a product pitched by an unsure salesperson? Would you be compelled to buy it or say "no" and pass? If you're like most people, the answer would be "no" and you'd keep your hard-earned cash.

Luckily, one of my co-workers educated me on the expectation game. One night, Natasha, a tall Russian blonde with big fake boobs, grabbed my hand, and boldly announced, "I like your butt. You are working with me tonight." This was my first corporate club in Manhattan. Natasha had a fairly strong Russian accent. I was brown, short, with real breasts and a round behind. I was unsure as to why she felt we were a good pair. Maybe she felt like our contrast was a good package. Or she felt bad for the new timid girl who was trying way too hard. Or maybe, she really did just like my butt.

I'm not really sure what made her choose me that night; I always worked alone. However, I went along with it as if I had no choice. She was confident and I could feel the power and momentum of her expectation. I honestly felt like a toddler trying to keep up with a fast walking parent. She'd approach customers, do a quick introduction and declare, "We dance for you now!" She'd start dancing and at first, I'd be so stunned (and waiting for the customers to protest), that she'd start taking my dress off for me, as she danced already topless. She'd have to break me out of my disbelief that it could be that easy to not only sell a dance but to sell a double dance.

I quickly caught on and began taking my own dress off without hesitation once she made the declaration. We danced and I was fascinated. I was failing at the expectation game when I was dancing solo. I was spending too much time (a song or two or three) chatting up customers and trying to feel them out, before timidly asking for the sale. Natasha approached already knowing she'd get the sale. Now, did we always get the sale? No. But that night, I saw way more yes's when I approached the customer like I had already won.

I also started doing this when I'd go into a new club to audition. I'd act as if I already worked there. I'd approach the door, talk to any staff that I encountered as if they were already familiar. I'd act as if I already belonged, chatting and joking around like I was with long-time friends. My disposition was confident versus being ridden with nervousness about whether I'd get hired or not. I also knew that they'd all be communicating with each other via earpiece. Better to have them chatting about the outgoing, friendly, and hopeful, than the scared one.

The first time I auditioned in Manhattan, I tried five or six clubs and got rejected by all of them. All of them said no. After my experience with Natasha, over time, I went from being nervous during auditions to having the confidence to expect being hired for the job that I wanted. With a shift in my mindset, I was able to get hired more easily. I wish I had known then what I know now. If you want to win, practice until you move with confidence. Expect that you will win. If nothing else, you won't win every time but your winning average will for sure greatly increase.

Is there a situation you have to go through on your journey towards your big goal that makes you feel uncomfortable? Are you an accountant, not obtaining enough customers? A PR rep, not securing enough press for your clients? A sales rep, not reaching quotas? For freelancers and artists, talking about money with clients to get paid fairly for your craft? We all have some area in our lives that make us uncomfortable. What's yours? What if you do an experiment and spend the next several times you do it, deciding to walk in, make the call, pitch the idea, negotiate confidently? You can practice for free. Do a phone call with someone you know who is doing the same thing you are doing. Practice on each other. Get feedback. Then write me and tell me what you learned.

"You get what you expect in life. Expect great things in life. Live your best life." - **Lailah Gifty Akita**

3) LOVE THE IMPERFECT SKIN YOU'RE IN

"Even the models we see in magazines wish they could look like their own images." - **Cheri K. Erdman**

One night, I watched a woman approach every guy as if she was the life of the party, bringing the party with her to them. She looked like so much fun, as she danced over to guys, arms up swaying to the music, with a huge smile. And guess what? She never got sent away immediately, even if she didn't ultimately get the sale. She maintained her joy no matter what the outcome of her approach was. When she heard no, she'd leave and continue the party dancing and snapping as she moved onto the next customer.

I started using a combo of Natasha's expect-to-win and this woman's "life of the party" approach. This became one of my introductions to club customers. I also used this approach in my auditions (for other clubs, bartending, and acting jobs). My theory became, show up and *do* the job. Don't audition. Introduce yourself to customer expecting them to say "yes." Don't hope or wish for it. In life, we get what we (often subconsciously) expect. And while approaching life as if you've already won doesn't guarantee a win every time, it sure does help us become more comfortable in our skin as we navigate the no's on the way to the yes's and ultimately towards self-defined success.

I'll tell you what else will get you comfortable. Walking around a club filled with scantily clad, mostly twenty-something-year-old women. Most women are conditioned to feel like our bodies are not in shape enough, especially if you're older and packing a few extra pounds. You can't survive in the club if you hold on to that lie and mindset. There are many pairs of perky breasts (real and augmented). The dim lighting of the club hides any trace of cellulite and other "imperfections" in the women around you. And so there I was, left with this false image of everyone else's "perfection," which brought to surface the "imperfections" I had in my head about my own body.

My breasts felt too small, my thighs felt too big, the stretch marks on my butt felt like too much, and even at a size 4, I felt huge next to size 2's and zeros. Going topless is a non-negotiable part of the job. So, night after night of baring it down to the G-string began to give me a level of body acceptance I had not expected. Simply put, I had to get over myself. There's no getting around it. Being a stripper means you must strip.

I worked in Manhattan and Las Vegas clubs, where everyone was rarely more than a size 4 or 6. There were plenty of size zeros. I also worked in dive bars and clubs in the New York City boroughs and New Jersey that hired bigger and smaller women alike. And regardless of your size, there was no rule that made anyone exempt from stripping off costumes.

There was a teeny tiny lady that worked at a dive bar that would seldom take off her costume. While I had no problem with it, apparently customers (and some other dancers) complained to the owner. She was told that she had to be topless at some point during her stage set. Then, there were signs put up in the dressing room about the club being a *topless* bar (the signs in the dressing rooms can fill a whole other book. So I will not digress). She left the club soon after that. The cool thing about stripping is that there's no shortage of places to get hired. Strip clubs are all over the place. I guessed that her not wanting to be topless had more to do with wanting more money for the privilege of seeing her nearly bare body than about her body hang ups. But who knows. The point is, all strippers gotta strip at some point. And I could've chosen to be endlessly tormented by showing my body or get over it.

- Our bodies are shaped how they are shaped.

- They change as we age.

- They change as we fluctuate up and down in size.

- They are what they are...and we only get one.

When the lights are on in the dressing room of the club, you begin to realize that like in magazines, the "perfect" body by "traditional beauty standards" doesn't exist either. In fluorescent light filled dressing rooms, after wipes have removed the foundation and other makeup, the imperfections that are invisible on the floor of a strip club clearly appear. Don't believe me? Do a Google search for before and after Photoshop pictures of models, actors, and other celebrities. It takes hours in a professional makeup artist's chair for these women to look like the image of perfection being sold to us. And after that, these images are edited with Photoshop. Even a regular working actor has blemishes removed and lines softened in their headshots. We can't have our confidence linked to the Photoshop version of ourselves and others.

Our bodies are perfectly imperfect, and true confidence is in embracing all of it – even the preconceived imperfections. This is a challenge because of all of the images we are constantly fed about fabricated beauty standards. We have to realize that we are reaching for something that isn't even real.

Whatever inner work we need to do to embrace our imperfections is mandatory.

For me, it was getting naked in front of strangers for years. For you, it may be therapy, mirror work (spending time in the mirror looking yourself in the eye), journaling or any combination of things that shift you to a place of gratitude, acceptance, and peace with and about your body.

One of my stripper friends had a brother who was a highly paid professional. His wife convinced him to pay for her liposuction surgery, where she promised to work out to maintain the "perfection" from surgery. I'm all for women doing whatever they choose to do with their bodies to make them happy. So, this is no indictment of plastic surgery. However, this woman was so disappointed that while she was smaller, her body was still shaped the way it was shaped. She never worked out to stay small and swiftly went back to the size she was before surgery. Her issue wasn't her size. She never learned to love the way her body was naturally shaped.

No matter what, I am never going to have a small behind or shapely calf muscles. I was teased as a child about my round butt. Now, women risk their lives getting shots to have their backsides look like mine. I also ran track for years. My calf muscles are just small. I'm thin. I have a scar from a surgery. I also have stretch marks and cellulite. I have accepted that I'm shaped the way I am. I love every stretch mark, cellulite dimple, and the jiggly bits because they're mine. It's what my body naturally does. I actually like the way I look naked more than the way I look clothed. The confidence that body acceptance brings can command a room. It is work worth doing. It is one of the secret ingredients to my confidence on any stage or in any part of life.

I learned that how we feel about ourselves has a HUGE affect on our overall beauty. There are plenty of pretty faces that no one wants to spend any time with. How do people feel after they have an interaction with you in the real world? What is the energy you intentionally bring into each space you enter? Do you decide to bring in the sunshine or be on the lookout for impending doom? We know the world is terrible. There are also a bunch of really great people in it. Are you demanding that other people treat you with care and respect but then berate yourself all day long? Are you working on having congruence of thoughts, desires, and love for ourselves imperfectly perfect? We all got things. We know America makes sure that marginalized groups get extra heaps of things. What do we do to shield ourselves away from it? Should we focus inward until it doesn't stop us from doing the work we would rather be doing? Do we set aside hours to work on our big goal the same way we spend hours arguing with strangers online? We get to keep some of our time for the express purpose of loving on ourselves. Can we commit to doing it until it is no longer uncomfortable but is also eagerly anticipate? I'd love to hear about the creative ways you come up with. Let's make a love yourself encyclopedia for the world.

"One day I had to sit down with myself and decide that I loved myself no matter what my body looked like and what other people thought about my body." - **Gabourey Sidibe**

4) JEALOUSY IS A SELF-PRODUCED SOAP OPERA

"The jealous are possessed by a mad devil and a dull spirit at the same time." - **Johann Kaspar Lavater**

I'll be honest...my brain has a really difficult time processing jealousy.

Stop and ask yourself: "How does hating on what this person has or has accomplished really serve my life?"

According to Merriam Webster, *jealousy* is defined as: a feeling of unhappiness caused by wanting what someone else has.

Working in strip clubs fixed any jealousy DNA I had in my spirit. On the outside, it looked like many customers had it all...but the things some of them were willing to do to get it all...well, I didn't understand and the multiple masks they'd wear reinforced my choice – that at all costs, I was willing to only be myself.

I learned so much while sipping champagne on the laps of businessmen discussing deals. One night, there were a group of men that came to the club for a dinner. Don't laugh, some clubs have really good food. And of course, we all hoped they'd go into VIP afterwards. We sat with them and chatted as they ate appetizers, steak, and sides. I ended up sitting with the loudest one in the group.

He was like a brash teenager in a middle-aged man's body. There were the things he said out loud, which were mostly obnoxious and there were the things he said in my ear, which were all fairly normal. We talked about his wife and how long they'd been together. He talked to me about what he loved about her. Hearing the things he said out loud versus what he said quietly to me was like interacting with two people in one body.

We all ended up going into VIP. The other ladies danced and entertained his peers. We sat and talked and joked around. It was fascinating to see the hoops grown men will jump through to close a deal to seem like one of the "cool kids," even if it went against their personal and marital values. I was fine with being paid to talk with him. My job was basically to be a body to block other strippers from approaching him. I got paid to be a stripper repellent.

Throughout my years in clubs, I learned that corporate America is filled with just as many insecure men as it is with people who are sincere, confident, and with integrity. When I started working in the clubs, I used to be jealous of the money many businessmen had. But soon I began to see what kind of personal compromises some had to make to have access to wealth earned in Corporate America.

The next stop for this group was going to be to a hotel room. There would be various sex workers for the group to hang out with. And as my client was leaving, he talked to me about staying loyal to his wife. I actually believed him because men have no reason to tell a stripper a lie (sometimes they were too honest with us) and he genuinely seemed to be in love with his wife. I've heard plenty of one-sided complaints about married life. And sometimes, I felt like I was leading a confessional or therapy session instead of giving lap dances. Just like this man, so many men were just pretending to be "one of the fellas." But then they would whisper in my ear that they didn't really want to be in the club, but it was part of work. This man was not interested in taking part in the hotel fun, but would go long enough to show his face and pay his portion for the outing. He pretty much paid me to keep other dancers at bay, but still create the illusion of having a doting dancer all to himself as well.

These types of interactions were jealousy reality checks as everyone has their path to walk towards wealth. And jealousy is fueled by the fear of scarcity. Just because someone achieves something, doesn't mean that they haven't made sacrifices and that there is not enough of that thing for everyone in the world going forward. This applies to material possessions, money, relationships, and anything else under the sun. One person winning doesn't limit opportunity for other people. Winning requires work – some enjoyable and some not so much. It becomes a matter of what work are you willing to put in to win your goal. But there is no deficit in opportunities if you open your eyes, dig in, and work smart.

Genuinely celebrate other people's wins… or just be distracted from increasing your own.

I used to work at a club in Las Vegas where there were certain ladies who refused to work the floor for $20 dances. They preferred to hunt for big payoff. They wanted VIP room spenders only. And it makes complete logical sense, right? Why waste time working harder, when you can wait and potentially earn more money working smarter?

I respected these women. I admired their hustle. However, I did not have the stomach to stand around waiting for The Big Ones. My energy would wane. I'd get anxious about if the Big Ones would show up for me that night. I was only working 2-3 nights on weekends. So, I preferred to work the floor with the mentality that it only takes one upgrade from a bunch of $20 dances to score a few hours in VIP. I could have been jealous of these women. Their tactic worked well for them. They usually did get The Big Ones (see Chapter 2 on expecting to win). Some of them had regulars, some of them paid the bouncers to tip them off to who the big spenders were, some of them just had excellent hustle and sales skills.

What would being jealous of their working style do for me? It would only distract me from doing MY work the way I did it.

I worked my way and they worked theirs. There were women who strictly worked in the club, women who were comfortable being paid to hang out at casinos or to be taken shopping by customers outside the club, and others who had no issue going to a hotel to work bachelor parties. What I knew for sure, is that everyone has a story and a reason behind what they did, and the way they would do it. For example, there was a woman who was supporting her whole family back in her home country. She worked six or seven nights a week. She had to maintain not only her living expenses in over-priced New York City, but also had to send money home for her whole family: parents, siblings, cousins, etc. She was under a great deal of pressure. From the outside looking in, it appeared as if she was always working and always making money, so her life must be easy and glamorous, right? Knowing her story changed that perception. I saw someone determined but burdened by the responsibility to earn as much as possible. The importance of her drive was in the strength of her why. It doesn't make any sense to judge or covet anyone for what they have. The way things appear on the outside aren't always the way things are behind the scenes. Like social media, curation versus real life existence, there is often more to any given story. I was there to make money, and create my own way, not expend energy uselessly coveting what other people had or how they got it.

If you want something that someone else has, put your head down and go work for it in your own way. Find your own hustle, use the principles you're learning in this book, and work them to the fullest extent. Often, instead of working towards a goal, we will spend time comparing ourselves to people who already have reached that goal. It is not useful. We have no idea what that person's full story is. What do you do when you want something?

a.   Think, why not me and write down some steps you could start to achieve it

b.   Seek out the help of a mentor who is where you want to be already

c.   Meditate on what it would feel like if you already had it

I am going to hope your answer is all of the above. Your ego may feel vindicated because of insults you were able to hurl at someone you're comparing yourself to, but are you any closer to your goal? Decide to focus on yourself and all of the things you've started and pick one to laser focus on until completed.

"I don't get jealous of people. Jealousy is such a waste of time because you're jealous of them, and they go about their lives and have a wonderful time, so what's the point?" - **Joy Behar**

5) BE PUSSY POWERED VS.

LEADING WITH PUSSY

"Thank you, Sacral Chakra for the free flow of feminine energy within and around me." - **Sacral Chakra Prayer**

Surprising to most, leading with pussy in the strip club doesn't get you very far. Pussy does not set you apart since almost every stripper in the club has one (I say "almost" because there were some gorgeous transgender strippers, who were highly successful, but that's a story for someone else to write).

Too many women assume that leading with pussy will keep men, or if you're a dancer, keep customers coming back for more. This is why so many men have sex with women, disappear, and the woman cannot figure out why. As a stripper, in order to get repeat customers, or to get a one-time customer to spend all their money on you, they needed to be engaged in a "sacral" way. I'm not saying that a woman has to have a time limit on when she chooses to sleep with a man. There just has to be a more binding relationship than just pussy whether you sleep together on the first date or fourth month of dating.

The sacral chakra is an energetic power source located near your womb area and is connected to your pussy. When you reduce your pussy to just carnal engagement, without acknowledging its spiritual and creative power, you disrespect and misuse that energy. Strong sacral energy is the difference between seeing a person, who has a sensual magnet that draws you close and vulgarity that lacks grace and therefore is a repellent.

Imagine your sacral energy as a battery that infuses your spirit with the ability to magnetize and enhance the curiosity of those you chose to attract. It can be used for business or pleasure by using different levels on the dial of the same power source.

To say, I will have sex with you is one thing. To have someone longing to know you more deeply because of how good they feel in your presence is another.

I was dating someone who I'd known since my teens. We were friends first and remained extremely close friends over the years. One day, while at a street fair, we met a woman with her group of friends. We had one of those random New York adventures, where we ended up partying and having late night/early morning breakfast with this group of women. Afterwards, we all connected on social media. And months later, this woman decided that she was interested in my friend, but she never bothered to ask if we were a couple.

Behind the scenes, she would pursue him privately, while publicly liking my posts and proclaiming that she wants to hang out with *me*. She never once mentioned that she liked my guy, but of course, why would she? Well, she was completely unaware that I knew what was going on the entire time. My guy and I began comparing notes and screenshots. I was shocked that someone could be so slimy. And he was insulted that she thought that he was as slimy as her.

She tried to lure him with invitations to topless video calls. She'd write to him about the sexual dreams she had of him. She bought him a Christmas gift and tried to use this as a lure too. He gave her my address to mail the gift.

She tried to get him to visit her on Christmas Eve and Christmas Day without success. We spent New Year's Eve together, and she still tried to get him to come see her New Year's Day. She doubled down in her pursuit of him, sending him music and pleading for them to speak. He'd been ignoring her and continued to ignore her. I posted a meme that said something to the effect of someone that really loves you will want you no matter what. She soon after liked a few pictures on his page.

Here's the kicker. He's single. We were broken up the whole time she was in pursuit of him, so she actually had a shot. But she kept behaving and embracing the side chick role, leading with just her pussy. She would've gotten so much further if she was truly tapped into her sacral power, because initially, he was attracted to her. However, her desperation and lack of confidence turned him all the way off. Sex and a spirit filled with sensual sacral energy are two different things.

Do you recognize it when you see it? Do you know people that have everyone in a room drawn to them as if under a spell? How do you fill a space with good energy? Even if you plan on being in the corner watching the action, can you feel when you have your sacral switch on? What gets that energy to simmer within you? When do you walk out the house feeling at your sensual best?

*"Sexuality is less about the actual act of having pretty good sex... much more about surrounding yourself with an ever-simmering sensual energy, pulsating just underneath your daily life and infusing almost everything you do." - **Sera Beak***

20 Day Challenge

Week 2 (Day 6 - 10) Go through the next five days seeking ways in which you can be of service, in both big and small ways, to the people you encounter as you go through each the day. At the end of each day, write down at least three acts of service you either witnessed or initiated. Feel free to elaborate more about it in your journal

Bonus: Save a dollar each day this week.

6) FEARLESSNESS IS A MYTH

*"To fear is one thing. To let fear grab you by the tail and swing you around is another." - **Katherine Paterson***

Courage is not the absence of fear. Just because someone looks brave, doesn't mean their fear has gone away. I've had close friends say to me, "Yeah... but you're not afraid to do things so..." That is not the truth. I still feel fear. In fact, I am terrified often. My life is filled with unknown factors. I've been a freelancer for almost two decades. I never know where my next check is coming from or how much it will be. I live in one of the most expensive cities in the world. And all of that remains scary somewhere in my mind.

As a performer, I am my own biggest critic. I fear not being good enough all the time. I've been a professional performer for almost three decades and still walk onto sets, into voice over booths or onto stages scared I won't be good enough and/or I'll lose the gig. But fear can be managed with focused effort. I've learned to jump into taking action despite fear being there. Also, none of those fears have ever come true no matter how many times they pop up. Luckily, I've never been so awful that I had to be replaced. I'm pretty sure you've found that many of your own fears are unwarranted as well. Think about it.

I've trained myself to be my own best friend in my head. When the fear and negative self-talk gets on the mic in my mind, I have programmed myself to simply say, "Thanks for your opinion, but I don't give a damn." I ask myself what I would say to one of my best friends in the same situation. Then, I use that encouragement to replace those fearful voices with truthful ones. I became a cheerleader for me.

It is also extremely important to have a support system of like-minded people, who can hear your truth, know when you are acting from fear, and also commend you when you are doing great work courageously. There is a way in which our self-critics can be harsher than the rudest strip club customer and we can't charge ourselves for an hour in VIP to make it sting any less. So, we also need friends to speak life into us and remind us of our greatness. Creating a support system is important because we all have good and bad days. Group Text/WhatsApp? FB Group? Weekly face-to-face meeting? Weekly Google Video Chat? Whatever works for you!

I want you to try this out for one day. Anytime that your inner critic starts to speak loudly, say "NO THANKS!"

Say it out loud or just firmly to yourself and then replace it with your own personal choice. Create a short phrase about a measurable goal, for example. Mentally hit the delete button on any thought that is limiting or unsupportive to you. If I find myself saying "eff my life," I immediately change it to, "Bless my life." Use this as a tool to drown out the useless negative voices in your head. It's one of my favorite techniques. I use it for fear and I use it on days when depression is winning but I still have to be out in the world functioning as usual. If I am repeating, "Everything always works out for me," whether I believe it or not, as my personal mantra, it speaks over my fear. I remember specific examples of when and how things have worked out for me from different points in my life. Then the fear shows up quieter, less intense, and may even feel like it's gone at some point. However, it never totally disappears in every aspect of life. And that's okay, because we can choose to use our own personal mantras or quotes, tap into or create other techniques that work for us to quiet our fear.

Fear is deceitful. It seldom tells us the truth. Fear is great when it's keeping us out of harm's way. However, fear is horrible when it prevents us from starting or trying something new. Fear can inhibit you from reaching a goal or go after something big and scary. Excuses are fears roommate. In fear, excuses mask themselves as good reasoning or being proactive. We have to create ways to remind ourselves that fear is not honest. Stopping to ask what is the worst-case scenario that could happen is one way to put our fears into perspective. Then the inverse. Stop and ask what it the best-case scenario from taking the scary actions. Is a made-up fear worth not achieving or going after that goal? Hopefully, not. While working through fear does not mean automatic victory, it still is valuable. Even if we do not succeed after working through our fears, we learn important lessons about how we can get to the destination. Every mistake and failure come with lessons that often cannot be learned any other way other than through experience. Having thick skin in the game is the thing that learning curves are flattened by.

With every growth spurt, there comes unknown horizons to scale. Welcome fear, or at the very least, learn to work alongside it. As long as we are trying to take our lives to higher heights, and find ways to build despite our fears, is one of our most useful skills. I'd say it is a very necessary skill to hone and polish. Every level brings on new fears. Life is like a video game where the higher you get, sometimes the challenges get bigger. Hopefully, we have grown enough to be able to scale challenges in a way that our past selves never could have conceived. If not, why?

If we keep having the same types of setbacks repeatedly, are we getting the lesson? Are we adjusting something before we go forward again? What are some things you thought about trying but let fear stop you instead? Can you choose to do one of them now? If fear allows you to stay in the same place, what can you do to change that? If the fear stops you, is that goal really meaningful to you? It may not be. The bigger your why, the better equipped you are for taking on the challenges along the way as life is happening. Every challenge isn't given a catastrophe level rating. Wanting to give up after a few tries and failures is a clue that it's not that important to you. What is? What is so important to you no challenge, even fear, can derail you from it?

Ask yourself right now... How would you live life if you ignored fear?

"But above all, try something." - **Franklin Delano Roosevelt**

7) LIFE IN THE ZERO FUCKS ZONE

"Do what makes you happy, be with who makes you smile, laugh as much as you breathe, and love as long as you live." - **Rachel Ann Nunes**

I began stripping in my mid-twenties. I did it off and on until I was about 40-years-old before I quit. In fact, I had my 40th birthday party at one of my favorite dive strip clubs, while working a shift. When I first started, like many strippers, I had delusions of grandeur that I would be one of those women, who stripped temporarily—who got in and out quickly. But I had too many conversations with veteran dancers within my first week of stripping that taught me very few women were in and out of the strip club industry fast. It was far more accurate to say that women were in and out, and in and out, and in and out again, before finally exiting for good. The women who were older and did extremely well, had this relaxed vibe about them. My twenty-something-year-old self couldn't figure out what made them so relaxed. I just knew the older women had this "thing" about them. I now call this thing, the "Zero Fucks Zone."

The Zero Fucks Zone is a glorious place, where we have freed ourselves from caring about what others think about us. There is an ease as we move through any space. It was a hard zone for me to arrive in. I was a people pleaser. I wanted everyone around me to be happy and happy with me. I always worried about being misunderstood. Perhaps, it stemmed from having very strict parents who left no room for negotiation. Things were done their way, period. And I avoided having my parents unhappy with me by any means necessary.

This spilled into my friendships. I had a really close friend, who was also a performer. We were together often. We took acting classes together. We partied together. I spent the night at her apartment many nights. She spent the night at my dorm so much that the cafeteria workers thought she was a student at the university. We made a name sign for her on our dorm door and the Resident Assistant for the floor would leave forms for her along with the rest of us. She had a fierce and willful spirit. When she wanted her way, she pushed hard for it. I often acquiesced. Whether I wanted to do something or not, I'd go along with her whims. She was very happy. I was not. But it made me really uncomfortable to disappoint my friends.

I started going to see a therapist for various reasons. One of the first things we delved into was the idea of setting boundaries and saying no. I'd never heard of setting boundaries and "no" was one of the hardest words for me to utter to someone I cared about. Very awkwardly at first, I started doing both of these things with her. Initially, she'd push back. I'd feel horrible. I felt like I was being wrung out from the inside. I was so uncomfortable with saying no and setting boundaries with her. Her hardcore push back didn't make it any easier. She gave me plenty of opportunities to practice. Like, anything new was challenging. I persevered and she finally got used to the new non-people-pleasing me. As did all my other friends.

Fast forward into my thirties, I was a boundary setting, hard-no-saying bodybuilder. I no longer felt bad about not doing something. I no longer cared if other people thought I wasn't a good person, because I knew I was a good person. I let go of the need to be understood. My opinion of myself is what mattered to me the most. I remember reading a quote from Wayne Dyer that said, "One of the highest places you can get to, is being independent of the good opinions of others." This was a valuable golden ticket. Being a stripper meant living with the stigma that comes with that label. I lived in despairing isolation to avoid being judged by others. I did not want to have my value reduced to this one word – a word which few had good things to say about. It took me being so depressed and overwhelmed by feelings of dreaded isolation that I checked myself into a psychiatric emergency room before I'd start on a true journey towards self-actualization.

I landed squarely in the Zero Fucks Zone. I no longer cared about what other people thought of me. If I can't call you on the phone when I'm having a bad day, I REALLY don't care about your opinion of me. The Zero Fucks Zone is freedom. You'll have so many fun, amazing adventures when you remove any fucks left to give from your life!

So, I'm asking you now… What would you try if you REALLY didn't care what others thought about you? Most likely, you wouldn't be swinging from the pole, but maybe you'd take yourself out to a beautiful dinner solo or travel the world alone. Would you finally go for that thing you're truly passionate about? Would you dress in clothes that make you feel like a powerful and amazing woman with no regard about what *they* say about you?

What if you tried and failed in front of everyone? In the zero fucks zone, failure is nothing more than information to use when we try again. Failure is an impetus to adjust and go forth anew. What others think of your failure doesn't factor into your decision about trying again. In the zero fucks zone, we realize that this invisible *they* are of no consequence to our real lives. Often, those who have time to judge are not doing much of anything in their own lives. These people tend to be the only ones that have hours to spend talking down about what other people are up to. Why would any fucks be wasted on *them*? I hear people talk as if the opinions of these imaginary "they" folks, have real power over any aspect of our lives. Thoughts that people have about us, positive or negative, do not have impact on our lives if we give their opinions zero weight. The naysayers are likely not a part of your target market anyway. Why base decisions on the opinions of those least likely to patronize your offerings to the world?

The possibilities are endless in here. Come on into the Zero Fucks Zone. It is a zone bereft of even an inch of a fuck to give. I know you're going to like it here! Choose to arrive here. The ride may be filled with turbulence but the landing will be the softest touch.

*"Nothing would be done at all if we waited until we could do it so well that no one could find fault with." - **John Henry**

I've created a virtual #ZeroFZone dedicated to women who are survivors of sexual violence. We are often affected in ways that cause us to care way too much about what other people think. Sometimes, we allow self-doubt and imposter syndrome keep us small. It is a closed group of like minded women ready to discover how to stop letting self-doubt stop them and start embracing their personal prowess. From time to time, I host a free live 5-Day Challenge where I teach you how to live in the Zero Fuck Zone. I also randomly pop up live from time to time too! Join me in the #ZeroFZone closed group on Facebook!

For those ready for an even deeper dive into having a mindset reset, I have a live online group program called S.T.R.I.P. Shift. It is a small group setting so that you can get all the focus that you need from me. Fill out an application to work with me one on one or in my group program.

8) TRUST FUNDS

"Lack of money is no obstacle. Lack of an idea is an obstacle." - **Ken Hakula**

There was a time when I would joke that stripping was my trust fund. I do not come from a rich family. When I wanted to do non-essential things, I sometimes would have to figure out ways to make it happen on my own. For instance, I wanted to do pageants as a teen, but I had no idea about the cost it would entail. And my parents did not waste money on frivolous things ever. A pageant, for sure, was frivolous. But when there's a will, there's a way. And it somehow popped into my head to be sponsored by my classmates. Then, I got a few bigger donations from a hardware store my parents' friend owned. Next, one of my mother's friends volunteered to make my dresses. When she wasn't able to, I'd borrow a gown from a store then return them like stylists do for shoots. I reached my sponsorship requirement one dollar and gift at a time. Admittedly, I had a longer list of sponsors than anyone else in the pageant. And I most definitely had sponsors who gave way smaller amounts. However, we were all in the same pageant, so I didn't really care about the number of sponsors it took. I reached the goal – to be part of the pageant.

A lack of money doesn't ever have to be a deterrent from doing something. Sometimes creativity creates the way. Pageants were one of my earliest lessons in how much single dollars can add up. Primitive crowdfunding, perhaps? Prelude to stripper dollars, maybe? Half kidding… but not really.

As long as we are alive and willing to be creative, we can figure out a way out of no way. I've come to learn that trusting you will be taken care of, coupled with a willingness to work smart (not hard) accomplishes most things. I've learned that there is a difference between hoping and knowing. Hoping means that on some level we expect may not happen. I leave those decisions to the Universe. In my mind, I know that I will manifest everything I need and much of what I want as well. One of the ways that has helped me trust this, is by releasing the desire for a specific result. We've heard this said. What we put it into practice often manifests in the most unexpected ways. They may not happen in the way we imagined. They may not happen in the timing we imagined. But there is definitely power in the release of how the result should look.

I'd set a weekly earning goal for my stripping work week. I also had a monthly goal. Sometimes, I could make my goal in two nights. Sometimes, it took six nights. Sometimes, I didn't make my weekly goal at all and owed the club money for house fees (as independent contractors we pay to rent the space). However, I very seldom missed that monthly goal. It almost always balanced out by the end of the month. After stripping for a while, I learned that the energy spent lamenting a bad night or week was wasted energy. By the month's end, I'd be near or surpass my goal for the month.

Does this mean that we always win? Hardly. Life will always be filled with wins and losses. I will keep reiterating this. We have to go forward in spite of this. It simply feels better to strut through the club (and life) as if everything is already sorted out. A relaxed state of mind tends to come up with solutions on the issue that needs solving. While a stressed state of mind tends to focus more squarely on the problem (often blowing it out of proportion). Though we cannot lose awareness of a challenge that needs solving, we can absolutely put more energy into the idea that there's a solution already there waiting for us to realize its existence. The inverse is counter-productive. Worrying often balloons the challenge to a greater size than it actually is. Therefore, the money we need to do everything we need to do and much of what we want as well, can be manifested with a sincere knowing and trust.

I would start my shift by watching the room. I liked to feel out the room's vibe before diving in. I'd decide if I was going to be quick with an introduction or risk taking a little more time to get to know the customer. The slow sell usually yielded the best return for me. However, sometimes the vibe would be so electric, I'd decide to go for the quick sell. On those fast-paced nights, when there was a fast turnover from customer to customer and group to group, making money would be in small continuous bursts. I'd trust whatever direction I was led to go in. Head next to the table to the right. Swing around and go to the table behind. Go left next time and try them over there. Life is no different. We all have a trust fund and ability to manifest abundance within. Often, if we take a moment to step back and take everything in first, look at a challenge from all angles, we can intuit how to move forward. What is the smallest next action we can take? Sometimes a quick bump and grind is required. Other times a slow burn will bring about a more beneficial outcome. When we trust that the answers on how to move forward will come, they present themselves to us faster and more clearly.

If we've lived life a couple decades or more, we've likely been met with a storm of challenges. It's also likely that we've gotten through and past most of them. At the time, it seemed like we would never figure it out. But we did figure it out. We often figure it out. Getting to the other side of things often leaves us wondering, "Why we ever worried in the first place?" How does it serve us to worry? How does it affect us to deal with finding the solution knowing somehow, you will sort it out? However, when the next set of challenges arise, we quickly forget. Going forward, can we work to remember that it is easier to get to the other side, trusting and knowing that it will work out in the end? The time will pass whether we worry or not.

Please trust. You got this!

"The key to abundance is meeting limited circumstances with unlimited thoughts." - **Marianne Williamson**

9) LISTENING

"There is as much wisdom in listening as there is in speaking—and that goes for all relationships, not just romantic ones." - ***Daniel Dae Kim***

Listening sometimes feels like a thing of the past. I live in New York City. We don't greet each other or make eye contact. We barely acknowledge the presence of others as we pass by millions of other New Yorkers each day. People everywhere seem to listen in on conversations only for the moment to talk more than they listen to the other person they are in conversation with. When I was on stage, I'd be on the lookout for someone who seemed to be very interested in me. I'm on stage so, of course, I'd be dancing for the whole room. However, when I would make eye contact with that person, the interaction would be his, all his. It would appear as if I was dancing for him and him alone.

Once I'd get off stage, I'd go directly to him. The thing that I was best at selling was great conversation, silly banter, and listening without judgment. I'd pay attention to everything he was saying. I'd create inside jokes for us based on what we talked about. I'd look him directly in the eyes. Whatever he wanted to talk to me about, I'd listen intently. No topic was off the table. I would create a conversation oasis where he could say all things about anything he'd never normally say out loud to anyone else.

One night I was working and I made friends with an older gentleman. He was in the military and had been to Afghanistan a few times. He wasn't buying dances, but he would tip me while we drank and talked. He told me about the things he saw while in Afghanistan. He talked about the challenges of being a high-ranking leader for men at war. He talked about the experience of having guns in his face. I stopped and sat listening to him in between hustling the room for dances and VIPs. I just listened. I was simply there to witness the stories of his experiences. It was intense. He had tears in his eyes at some points. I had to give myself breaks by peddling sexy dances to other customers. I will not go into all the deep details, but there are probably few places someone with his level of clearance could openly talk. I made more money from him than anyone I took my clothes off for that night. And all I did was listen with an open heart and open mind. No judgment. All listening.

When we work on being present with the people we have dialogues with, magic happens. Listen without expecting to talk about yourself. Listen with the only intention of being an ear for them. Do this with people you do business with in life. Do this with the service people you encounter as you go through life. Do this with anyone you have interpersonal relationships with in life. Part of being an actor is active listening. Imagine watching a show where the actors check out until their next line. Imagine the characters having no reaction to what the other characters say. The scenes would be flat and not very entertaining. Imagine watching a dancer so uptight about choreography, you can see them counting steps versus dancing and entertaining. Life is the same. You sacrifice depth when you don't listen and aren't fully present.

I would listen to the porters in the club. To some of the dancers and other staff, they seemed like invisible workers. Yet, without them, club life would be messy. All the spilled drinks, broken glass, toppled food and any myriad of other jobs they do for the club, are very important. They seemed to walk around doing their work largely ignored. I'd make it a point to stop and say hello as I pass. Wherever I encounter service providers, I try to spend some time asking about their shift or their day.

I've had the most fascinating conversations in taxi cabs. Many of the drivers I speak to are also artists. They drive to earn money while pursuing their passion. We often end up sharing war stories of adventures in living an artist's life. In New York City, there are people from all over the world driving cabs. I listen to these people brag about their kids, how many hours they work, and their reasons for doing this work. Once a cab driver burst into laughter after we started talking. He told me that it had been seven hours since he actually spoke to someone.

I don't listen to people expecting anything in return from them. There's something that feels good about not focusing on oneself. My parents taught me, mostly through behavior, that we should always be nice to the people in our lives. I find that listening to someone has a soothing effect. Not everything that we do has to be about getting something out of the exchange. Not every conversation needs to have heavy responses from us. We can listen without volleying for our next time to talk. Too often we listen only to find the moment that we can jump in with our thoughts and never fully listen to the person we're in conversation with. Sometimes, we can just take a moment to add more goodness into the universe by quietly bearing witness to someone else.

Do you listen during conversations or are you just waiting for a break so you can be heard? Are you focused on the people that you are talking to or staring at your phone and only half listening? How can we be more present in conversations with the people we come across as we go through life? Do you allow yourself to hold space for someone without having to interject yourself into it? It's an interesting gift to both the talker and the listener.

"Listening is a magnetic and strange thing, a creative force. The friends who listen to us are the ones we move toward. When we are listened to, it creates us, makes us unfold and expand." - **Karl A. Menniger**

10) ASK FOR WHAT YOU WANT

CLEARLY

"Asking for help with shame says: You have the power over me.

Asking with condescension says: I have the power over you.

*But asking for help with gratitude says: We have the power to help each other." - **Amanda Palmer***

I hear so many people say that they have a hard time asking for things. Walking the floor of a strip club every night, ya gotta ask! You could wait to be approached. However, the only way to make money in a strip club is to ask for what you want. Most of the time, it's asking for a dance or to spend time in the VIP room or a bottle of some adult beverage or another. The first time I had to ask for money, straight up, no chaser, I was so uncomfortable – deeply uncomfortable. I don't have the words to describe the sense of foreboding I experienced the first few times.

The way that I asked for the sale when I was uncomfortable with the ask was terrible. Immediately, my thought would go to what a large amount of money I was asking for. That seemed like too much to spend at one-time on something like a VIP Room visit. It seemed like a waste to me initially. If you've ever done sales, then you know the difference between selling a product you believe in and one you don't. Me asking for dances was like me saying, "You don't really want a lap dance, do you?"

I grew up in a house where wasting money was a sin. I got good at not asking for anything or expecting no if I did ask for anything from my parents. As a child, I had no idea how limited a budget my parents were on taking care of my sister and me. As children, my sister and I felt like our parents were doing great financially; to us, we had everything we needed. But now as an adult, we marvel at how well our parents managed with what money they did have. We went on vacations, there was always food, utilities were never disconnected, etc. My parents come from extremely humble beginnings. Wasting money was not something I grew up learning to do. Quite the opposite. But then, I would think about the value of my time. I was providing a service. I'm great at creating a fantasy that is pleasing to look at (for some). I'm pretty good at being interesting, no pressure company. When at work, I was willing to talk about ANY topic. I can talk about anything for at least a few minutes at a time. I would take my time getting ready. The preparation would begin at home and often took more time once arriving at the club. I worked out five days a week. I often smell like a tropical oasis. I was worth the fee for all I provided.

What people think happens in strip clubs is that strippers waltz in, have thousands of dollars tossed at them and they skip home. Easy money. What actually happens is we approach customers while they are seated either alone or in a group. If in a group, we have to hope we pick the one that would want to spend some time with us individually or the one who controlled the Bachelor's money. If alone, we have to hope who we approach finds us attractive and/or interesting. Most of the time, they do not. A shift at a club is filled with ask after ask, and sometimes getting turned down. Yet, we keep asking. While we may not get everything we ask for, we get a greater percentage of what we asked for than we would if we didn't ask at all.

Remember the 10's waiting to be asked while watching Plain Jane work the room in Chapter One? As we walk through life, the same is also true. Asking, very clearly, for what we want is important. I think this is especially the case for women socialized to not "be difficult." This is a ploy to keep women quiet and in check. How else will we get what we want? I'm actually sincerely curious about what makes people awkward about simply asking for what they want. It's quite the cycle when a person does not ask for what they want. They succeed in getting the insufficient amount they asked for, which is nothing. Then, the person is resentful that they didn't get what they really wanted (which they didn't ask for). Your value as a person is beyond any dollar amount, therefore, ask for what your time and skills are worth. If there is no budget for what you are doing, say no.

What do you have to do to feel worthy of whatever "the big ask" is for you? In relationships, do you let your partner know clearly what you need and want? Or do you allow yourself to feel unsatisfied to spare someone else's feelings? With the people who are your friends, are you clear with what you want? Do you say yes because it seems like it would be easier to go along to get along? The outcome leaves you unhappy and the other party is being lied to. Who benefits? No one. If we really think about it, it is the height of arrogance to think that our ask is so magnanimous that it will crumble someone. It is also the height of low self-esteem to think that not asking somehow makes us morally superior to those who do ask for what they want. We must develop thicker skin around the possibility of being told no to our ask and continue to ask anyway. Why would we let someone who didn't follow through when they said yes initially, crumble us? They too thought that it was just easier to say yes so as to not cause any conflict. See how this works on all sides? Not speaking your truth ends up being more exhausting than easier. Just as I needed to feel worthy that I could make a certain amount per hour. I started expecting people to say yes to whatever I was asking them to buy in the club. I, in turn, became willing to ask for what I wanted in life or I'd simply walk away from the offer.

Asking for what you want can even sometimes spark some creative solutions where everyone wins. I sometimes had customers who didn't want to pay the additional fees that come with a VIP Room: room fee, bottle fee, tips to waitress, and security, all on top of my fee as dancer. One night I was sitting with a guy and his two friends. Each friend had a lady with them. Though we all were working alone, we became a team. We stepped away to "go to the bathroom." We collectively decided to ask for only our dancer's fee to stay on the floor with them for an hour. They agreed. They got our uninterrupted attention for an hour. The six of us hung out, laughing, with storytelling sprinkled between the dance. At the end of the hour, everyone was happy. Asking for what you want doesn't have to be a hard or difficult thing. The ask can be adjusted. You know what you're willing to compromise and what you're not before asking. So, just ask for it. Say a big scary number. Write out and repeat what your rate is [big scary number] until you can say it as if it's not a big deal. Be willing to negotiate. Asking for what you want should be a matter of fact. Your level of self-worth is priceless. Simply ask.

Do you only contact people when you want something? That's one way to get a no. Do you attempt to have the ask be mutually beneficial? Someone choosing to say yes to you does not mean that you owe them something. However, we tend to be creatures of reciprocity naturally. No one can force you to do anything. Are you choosing to believe that you will be in deep debt if you ask and accept help? When you help people to you think, "Oh yeah, they're in debt to me now!" I'm guessing that you don't. Even if you are a woman accepting help from a man, you do not then owe them anything but gratitude and a special place in your heart for having your back. You likely will have their back when they need you. Why would we assume the negative about someone offering help? They have the ability to say no. How can we raise our belief in how valuable we are so that no ask seems too big?

"State what you want, and go for it, don't refuse yourself a request you did not make."

*- **Bangambiki Habyarimana***

11) SINCERITY SELLS

"Sincerity makes the very least person to be of more value than the most talented hypocrite." - **Charles Spurgeon**

The entire fantasy of the strip club is based on a sexy woman being super interested in you. It creates an interesting challenge. Everyone who walks through the door is complicit in what is happening. So, how do you sell this in a way that doesn't feel manufactured? Sex doesn't sell (it was illegal in the clubs I worked at. I have always been terrified of police), but sincerity does. Finding some kind of sincerity for the exchange is important. I'd listen to customers at the onset of our conversation. I'd hope to hear at least one thing that we both liked. I could always create alliances with customers from my home state. Maybe we had nothing in common but he was really into something unique that peaked my interest. I wouldn't have to feign interest as I asked questions about it. As we got to know each other, I'd build rapport by finding at least one real way to connect with him. At any given time, a large club can be filled with eighty dancers or more. If you weren't sent away right away, what would make them want *you* to stay?

There would be some nights when I really wasn't into it. I'd do my best to run on autopilot. I'd typically get one of two reactions on those nights. The "Oooh she's good!" with the subtext of: she's a pro and not for real. Or simply a "No, thank you." I hardly ever did well on nights when my head wasn't in it. I'd go from making each encounter new and fun to trying to do it by route. The difference energetically is easily felt. Even if a person doesn't believe in things like energy, it is there. The proof is in the results. People can feel dishonesty. When others can feel your sincerity, it makes such a difference in the interactions you have with that person. There were some ladies whose persona was so over the top perky, I would wonder if they'd be exhausted by the time they got home. It's so much easier to just be who you are or at least a real aspect of who you are. Become curious about the people with whom you choose to have conversations with.

I once went to a dinner with a partner of mine. Everyone there was there for the purpose of introducing people at the table. Potentially, these connections could lead to business collaborations. Perhaps, someone at the table could help connect the dots to what someone else was working on accomplishing. I was very quiet at the table. Everyone at the table knew I didn't have anything that they wanted, so they had no problem ignoring that I was even there. What I observed around that table was a group of adults sharing a meal and every individual trying to get their personal agenda across. Everyone was all smiles. Many funny anecdotes were told. However, the conversation was one of the most disjointed conversations I'd ever heard. No one was really listening to anything other than for a moment of silence to break in with their agenda item. My face was neutral but internally my thoughts just kept swirling on how disconnected these people were from each other, while all were fishing to benefit from each other's connections. I wanted to record them, so that I could play it back for my partner later.

Nothing ever came out of that dinner for my partner. Nothing much ever came out of these dinners he went to. However, if this one was the prototype for the types of dinner meetings he was having, I understood why they never lead to concrete deals. No one at the table was sincerely interested in each other. The only interest they had in each other was what the other person could do for them. This doesn't make for a good foundation in friendships, personal or business relationships. I started calling these appointments "meetings to nowhere." They led to nowhere because no one was there for the purpose of benefiting anyone but themselves. Perhaps, everyone thinks that they're an actor, but they're not. Sincerity is palpable. It has a draw. Sincerity sells. Insincerity repels.

Stripping gave me many hours of practice at sincerely becoming interested in strangers. Do you pretend to like someone when you don't? Do you speak your truth more often than not? Can you find something that you are sincerely curious about in any new acquaintance? Do you surround yourself with people who are also sincerely interested in you? It goes both ways. You deserve sincerity too.

"Sincerity is the virtue of the righteous, the trait of the honest, and the most prized asset of the successful. Any act or deed, which is backed by earnest feelings of sincerity, is bound to be a success." - author unknown

12) SAVE FOR A SUNNY DAY

"Most of the shadows of this life are caused by our standing in our own sunshine." - **Henry Ward Beecher**

We've all heard the saying, "Save for a rainy day." What kind of motivation is THAT?! Is the only reason to save money because things are bound to go wrong? It's life. Things happen. We all know this. However, if the only reason people are saving money is for tragedy, why save? What if people chose to save for a sunny day? One of the things I love to do is travel. As a freelancer, I can choose to get on a plane, train or in an automobile on very short notice. It gives me such pleasure to wander aimlessly around a country I've never been to before. I love eating at the local eateries and staying in residential neighborhoods. I want to experience life in these places. I save money to do that. Luckily, as a performer, I get to travel the world for work. However, sometimes, I may just want to wander to a new place just for the sake of satisfying the wanderlust inside of me. We all probably have something that we'd love to get more opportunities to do. Why don't we save for that? I live a fairly cash based life in terms of my spending habits. If I can't pay for it in cash, I'm not getting it until I save up for it. Therefore, I have to save for everything that I want to do. Due to not working on a set income, I find it easier to separate my money by percentages. A percentage of my earnings goes towards doing something that I want to do just for fun. The unexpected can happen at any time in life, which makes it especially important that we spend some portion of our lives just enjoying and playing. It makes getting through the challenges of life so much easier knowing that life isn't only about putting out fires or managing the mundane. Life should also be about moments of fun for fun's sake. For me that means having more experiences than things. The larger bulk of my income certainly goes towards necessary expenses like rent, food and other monthly bills. I put aside money for the serious adult life things too, like investing and retirement. When I was a newbie in Manhattan clubs, an experienced stripper told me to learn about investing, read about it, save some of the money I was making for investing. I listened. However, a portion of the money we earn has to be put aside for a sunny day.

How much one should save for a sunny day varies person to person and it may take some longer than others to save up for their goal. However, it happens with consistency and discipline.

It takes serious discipline to keep each segment of savings and money management for its intended purpose. We live in a credit card society where some people choose to live above their means and then have to play catch up. If we all made sure that some portion of our money, even if it is one dollar at a time, was saved for a sunny day, our quality of life would feel much better. We have to come up with creative solutions to deal with life's challenges. Never use your sunny day fund for anything other than a sunny day. It could be money to blow on magazines that you can sit in the park and read. It could be for a vacation to a different place or a staycation. It can be for dinner and a show. It can be something large or very small. It just has to be paid for in cash and has to bring you joy. No matter what your income level is, some percentage of what you earn has to bring you happiness. Otherwise, life is just being lived and experienced as a never-ending chore. When life is only a never-ending chore, there is no space for dreaming. There needs to be space created either for the things you love to do and/or to sit in peace and figure out what you may want to do. Do you want a larger goal to work towards? Maybe you are happy right where you are and are on the right path for what you aim to achieve. Do you want to build a better mousetrap? Are you happy working for your employer or at least compensated enough for you to enjoy your life while your work builds someone else's company? Or your story could be that you'll stay in the job you're in to reap the benefits of a retirement income. Entrepreneur or employee, saving money for a sunny day very much improves your quality of life. We live in an all or nothing world. We tend to think that if we can't fly first class to Hawaii to stay in a five-star hotel then we just can't travel. If we are barely making it to get all the bills paid, we seldom think of the *small* ways we can love on ourselves doing something that will both make us smile for a moment and not stress about the amount spent on it. Our obsession with social media causes many people to get into the compare game. We know little of the back stories to many of our online "friend's" lives. Luxury to me may be buying a book at the big used bookstore here in New York City. Luxury may be a night home watching something fun while having my favorite snack. For someone else, it may be something more glitzy that fits into their budget. We sometimes allow someone else's curated version of life make us feel badly about our own lives. We only know the full stories for a few of our real-life friends. The total picture is always less shiny than the images online. Your life is being built by you, for you. The experiences of others do not factor into yours. Save for *your* sunny day. Let other people enjoy their sunny day.

Did you know that you can have many accounts at the bank? You can have one labeled for specific goals, a separate one for travel, one for saving up enough to invest, etc. Consistency is more important than quantity when saving. It adds up a lot more quickly than we think. Discipline and consistency will help us no matter what financial level we are at. If you can only save a quarter a day, do it. Choose whatever amount is comfortable for you that doesn't put you in financial distress. I hear so many people say I need my entire check, there's nothing left to save. If you have to start saving a quarter a month, do it. Create the habit of saving in general, especially saving for a sunny day. As William Shatner once said, "If saving money is wrong, I don't want be right."

Many of us were not given a financial education. Do you decide before the check is cashed, how it will be spent? It's a trap to get into the habit of spending everything we make. How much can you comfortable save each month? A quarter, a dollar, twenty dollars, fifty or more? Can you commit to making this a new habit? Can you think of the money you save the same way you treat a bill that has been paid? Will you think of your saved money as spent and not an option? Will we commit to using your sunny day fund only for something no matter what life throws our way? How else do new habits form? How can we break the financial patterns that do not serve us well?

"If money management isn't something you enjoy, consider my perspective. I look at managing my money as if it were a part-time job. The time you spend monitoring your finances will pay off. You can make real money by cutting expenses and earning more interest on savings and investments. I'd challenge you to find a part-time job where you could potentially earn as much money for just an hour or two of your time."

*- **Laura D. Adams***

13) OUR COMPLEXITIES

COMPLETE US

"Abandon the urge to simplify everything, to look for formulas and easy answers, and to begin to think multidimensionally, to glory in the mystery and paradoxes of life, not to be dismayed by the multitude of causes and consequences that are inherent in each experience – to appreciate the fact that life is complex." - **M. Scott Peck**

None of us are typical. We all look different. We all have different opinions. We all were raised to believe different things. Then, we all head out into adulthood and have our own personal set of experiences. All of these things color who we are. Some of the things we were taught growing up, we keep with us for our whole lifetime. Other things, we may decide no longer work for us. Even if people grew up in the same household to be the same, each individual's experience is different. Yet, so much conflict comes out of people wanting other people to see things the same way they do. This is the impossible dream.

The saying "Everybody Has a Story" is so very true. I've had conversations that were the wildest with customers who looked like the most conservative beings. I had a guy that would come in dressed in a business suit, briefcase, khaki trench coat, and a clean cut. He was on a mission to find a Black woman who would strap on a dildo and have sex with him. I've had that same type of man dance in my spandex, sparkly, pink stripper gown after a hard day on Wall Street. There was a regular customer I had, who was a blue-collar worker, father, mousy looking guy, who would like me to put makeup on him and call him by a feminine name. He was straight. He was also one of the nicest guys I'd met; we always had so much fun.

I've had some of the most intellectual and heartfelt conversations with drug dealers, who were dressed in hip-hop attire. These men would tell me about what creative passions they wanted to do more of. So many of these guys just wanted to relax, laugh, and have fun. This is universal. They enjoyed having the expendable income to throw at strippers (figuratively and literally). I too, have seen my fair share of bratty rich kids, celebrity, rock star behavior. I've spoken to people who are legends in their fields and are really kind to people affirming that we're all just human beings. Sometimes, the stories of our lives come together in ways that make us really good people. Other times, those stories make us villains. And sometimes, those evil villains end up with a lot of power. I learned through countless conversations that so many of us are letting our inner child run the show. Some of us cling to the victim story of all the wrongs that have happened to us all the way into the senior stages of life. These types of people often were the ones who thought they deserved more for doing the less. Yet, they make no actual action or steps towards improving or becoming of greater worth.

Then, I'd have experiences with the people who are constantly looking for ways to be better. I've met many men who enjoyed going to strip clubs who were this way. They were cool with going out alone to a place where the ladies would strike up a conversation with them. The societal pressure of being the alpha male in terms of introductions was reversed. They would come into the club just to have conversations with the dancers. They unequivocally refused to get dances. You couldn't even give away a dance to them for free. They also tended to come back on a semi regular to regular basis. These types of people always felt like they're successes were almost unwarranted. They often seemed as if they thought they'd be discovered as a fraud at any second. People who are the most deserving seem to be the least likely to believe themselves to be of as high a worth as they truly are.

Working the floor of a strip club, you hear countless stories. Some seemed true, some false. I had a guy who came into the club after 2:00 AM one night. He was telling me about his life as a hitman. I'm more inclined to think he was one of New York's method actors working on a role. Method actors attempt to live the actual life of a character they are preparing to play. Maybe he just felt like saying he was a hitman that night. I'm not really open to the idea that a hitman announces he's a hitman. No one ever came in with exactly the same story either. My job wasn't to try to convince the customers to see things my way or convince them to be truthful. My job was not to judge who they chose to be in that moment. What I did do was bear witness to a million tales. Some were funny. Some were sad. None were alike. A decade of bearing witness to so many stories in an arena where numerous topics were up for conversation, made me realize that life is seldom simple. There are so many twists and turns that our individual journeys can and do take. We can choose to stand back and be an observer, rather than always being in someone's face trying to change them or get them to see things our way.

Can we allow for there to be nuance? Can we allow for opinions to be just that? Can we think about things in our own lives that from the outside looking in looks one way, but the full story would reveal it to be different? Are we able to be less quick to judge people without knowing their full story?

"A man should not strive to eliminate his complexes but to get into accord with them: they are legitimately what directs his conduct in the world." - **Sigmund Freud**

14) IT'S JUST NOT PERSONAL

"Don't take anything personally. Nothing others do is because of you. What others say and do is a projection of their own reality, their own dream. When you are immune to the opinions and actions of others, you won't be the victim of needless suffering." - **Don Miguel Ruiz**

I tell myself often: "It's not about you, Essence." It's so easy for our egos to have us believe that everything is about us. We get so comfortable in our everyday existence sometimes that we forget other people are living different realities from our own. If someone does or says something, we jump to conclusions and take it personally. We scroll by a post on social media and immediately think it is about us. The fact of the matter is that people are so engulfed in their own lives, that they really are not thinking about us as much as our ego would lead us to believe. As a member of several marginalized groups, society does plenty that is offensive and discriminatory towards me. If I sought them out, there would be countless offenses that would present themselves several times in a day that I could call out and/or catalog. It would make me feel insane.

The floor of a strip club is no different. The majority of the time, I worked in predominantly white corporate clubs. There were always more blondes than anything else represented among the dancers. Some women badly damaged their hair from dying it blonde. However, they swore they made the most money that way and wouldn't stop. I am quite easily the opposite of a tall, wispy, thin, white blonde. I am a short, Black, curvy, dark haired woman. I would hear things all night that could be considered insulting. Many were probably not intended as such but numerous were. Taking anything said to me too personally would throw me off my game. By not taking anything personally, I'd arrive to the person or people who wanted to spend time and money on me in an upbeat mood.

Think of the missed opportunities that would happen if we were going through life constantly taking things personally. Imagine life choosing to let the small things roll off your back. If nothing else, the benefit is in the fact that you are in a happier state more often. People like to be around happy people, not people pretending to be happy. There is no way to be happy all the time. But it is very possible to choose to be happy most of the time. I live managing dysthymia depression. I know quite a lot about being very down. There has been clear evidence that when I was really happy, I made the most money. People come into a club to escape real life. It's a place they come to relax and have fun.

Imagine having more happy moments in your everyday life. What would life be if you were one of those happy spirits? How do we foster a genuinely happy spirit? One way is living the life you really want to live or get as close to it as possible. If working a great corporate job during the day so that you can live comfortably also means you can make time to paint, you do that. If you have the spirit to manage a freelancer's existence more than you value predictable income, do that. Perhaps, you are more the entrepreneurial type. Start a business. What work do you need to do on yourself for yourself? Do it. Anytime you feel like convincing someone else of your opinion, instead do something towards your own growth. Read everything you can. Learn new things all the time. Study cultures that are different than your own. Develop interests that make your heart sing. Learn more about yourself and what makes you tick. Try doing new things even if they scare you, *especially* if they scare you.

Therapy. That's a complete thought and a full paragraph. Do it. It is worth the effort it takes to find someone that is a match. You deserve it to yourself to clear up or process anything that may be stopping your growth, especially if you have been through any type of trauma.. I know how gloriously good it feels to tell someone off. It is ego candy. I certainly have had many moments when my ego luxuriates in going for the intellectual kill of someone who has insulted me. I once had an older white customer at a club scream out, "Your hands are too dry. I need to believe you live a pampered life!" I got up and said in his ear, "Everyone in this club is too young and too beautiful to ever be attracted to someone that looks like you. Enjoy the rest of your evening!" I smiled and walked away giggling to myself. If only I could do that in the real-world knowing security was on hand.

At the end of the day, though, the only person's opinion of you that really matters is your own. There is no way for anyone to know the ins and outs of your story and be able to form a fully accurate picture of who you are. I apply this to positive and negative comments alike. Compliments are lovely. More ego candy, please! I sincerely say, thank you. However, at a moment's notice, that person's opinion of me can change. Therefore, I don't put much cache on compliments or insults.

I see people waste a good portion of life trying to get other people to see things their way. Why? How can there be only one way for everything? How can you be right on all topics for everyone? What you choose for yourself is right for you. It is not universally good. End of story. Whether others label it as positive or negative, is a matter of outside opinion. Remember, the fucks we no longer give? I am no longer concerned about what you think of me. I refuse to allow other people to shake my peace of mind. I am quite capable of doing that all by myself. I have no need to outsource that activity. If people want to spend their copious free time talking badly about you, LET THEM. Be too busy building and living the life of your deliberate creation to notice or care.

Move through life looking for those people who are going to uplift you. Find your tribe. Surround yourself with people on the same trajectory as you. Surround yourself with people that are just as happy about your wins as they are their own. These types of people and experiences are much easier to manifest when you're not spending the bulk of your day taking things that people say to or about you personally. If I'd have allowed the microaggressions, macroaggressions, and direct insults I heard from customers affect my peace of mind, that would have hindered my ability to earn. Outside of the club, it would hinder my ability to manifest and attract the people that are about reciprocity when it comes to true friendships, cheerleaders, and support. Some things planted sprout, others don't. Just keep planting.

Are you the type of person who gets along with most people you encounter? Is it usually just a matter of time before you end up in a conflict with the people you encounter? Do you cling to being justified in a conflict? Do you spend time in debates over the opinions of others whom you will never change? Do you remind yourself that most people who are constantly in conflict are conflicted inside? It very rarely has anything to do with you personally. Do you nurture your real relationships (professional and personal) so that they span decades?

"My feeling was, you plant some seeds. If they grow, great; if they don't, you don't take it personally. Not my problem; I just kept planting. Just like a farmer." - **Hank Haney**

15) DARE TO SUCK

*"I don't divide the world into the weak and strong or the successes and the failures and those who make it or those who don't. I divide the world into learners and non-learners." - **Billi Lim***

This lesson came first to me from a theater teacher in college. It has served me well many times in life. When I first started working in clubs, I remember the uncomfortable feeling I had in my stomach every night. Later on, into dancing, there would be nights where I was actually excited to get to work, so that I could be that "fun, life of the party, work persona" lady. The only way I was able to get from the awkward, uncomfortable woman trying to sell dances, was to keep doing it. Several nights a week, I'd show up and try to do better. I had to get over the fact that I was not an expert at this. I knew nothing about the inner workings of a strip club before working in one. How could I expect to be an expert instantly?

I had to be willing to be bad at it until I got better. I love learning but I also despise learning curves! I just want to be able to know something or how to do something quickly. Unfortunately, the only way that I have ever learned how to do anything was to dare to suck at it first. If there was a way to avoid this, I would have figured it out and this section would be different. It took me trying and failing over and over again at selling dances and VIP rooms to get better at it.

It took me twenty years to feel like I could say out loud that I was a good actor. If I could bury videos from the first times I did burlesque, I would bury them deep. There is no shortcut to becoming better at something. Almost anything that we want to learn and excel at, we have to do over and over and over again. Fear prevents so many people from improving their lives. Fear stops people from trying new things. Fear stops people from ever beginning and leaves them always in the, "What if…?" Sometimes the "What if…?" is audible in our minds, other times it is not. It's still there though. It lingers in our spirits leaving us with a feeling that there must be more to living life than a mundane day-to-day existence. However, most people would rather excel at mediocrity because it's familiar than daring to suck at something new.

The reason why the older strippers on the floor were able to make money with ease is because over the years they moved from the sucky stage into sage stage. They have the ease of experts now. I would be terrified every single night in the beginning of my stripping career. I had to struggle to work while scared. I stripped for about two years before it became fun. After two years of working, I finally felt like I was in my own type of flow at work. I was willing to keep showing up and going out there being bad at it until I wasn't. There are probably areas in everyone's life where if they were willing to be bad at something, they'd discover something new that they'd be on fire to keep trying until they too had the ease of experts. Unfortunately, the majority of people are not willing to do that. The things that scare them that they could get good at, they never even attempt. Imagine going through life letting the imaginary story you've told yourself stall you from even trying? Imagine being more comfortable with the mediocre and mundane simply because it's familiar? Imagine getting to the end of your life with a gnawing feeling that you could have served some higher purpose or, at the bare minimum, had more fun and fulfilling moments? We live in a world where life unexpectedly ends for any number of reasons. How would you rather spend your days of life? No one ever said that it would be easy. It won't be. However, when life makes your heart sing, the work is worth it. Be intentional about the life you are creating. Take the lessons from all the bumps and keep going. Dare to suck.

How has not daring to suck stopped you from pursuing something new? What are the things you enjoy today that you initially sucked at? What makes you willing to take a risk and be bad at something while working on getting good? Can we agree that progress over perfection is a good motto to try on for size? We sucked at walking at first but we kept trying. How can we find the resolve of a child learning to walk, where all we know is to get up again?

"When you take risks, you learn that there will be times when you succeed and there will be times when you fail, and both are equally important." - ***Ellen DeGeneres***

21-Day Challenge

Week 3 (Day 11 - 15) Go through the next five days of this week choosing to only take part in positive self-talk. Become your own best friend in your mind. As a tool, create your own mantras. One of my favorites is: "Things always work out for me." You may find it more useful to mantra around a step you want to take this week: "I will complete 10 emails to potential customers, gigs, etc by Friday at 5pm." Focus on actions you can take versus that non cheerleader in our minds. Anytime those negative voices get loud in our heads, we can simply repeat our mantras to drown out those negative lies. In the evening do a short meditation using this mantra or use silence. Meditate for as long as you would like but make it at least five minutes. Set a timer. Let your thoughts happen and focus on your breathing. You may also use the guided meditations that came with the bonuses of purchasing this book.

Bonus: Save a dollar each day this week.

16) COMMUNICATE WHAT

YOU DO NOT WANT

*"Daring to set boundaries is about having the courage to love ourselves even when we risk disappointing others." - **Brené Brown***

I always hear people talk about how horrible stripping is for women. It objectifies women. It damages women in x, y, and z ways. I'll never be one to say that stripping is a great job for everyone. In fact, I'm likely to attempt to talk people out of choosing it at all. I do the same with acting hopefuls. Both of these jobs come with serious challenges that are not for everyone.

However, it was in clubs where I got priceless practice in communicating clearly what I did not want. You can imagine the types of boundaries some customers attempted to cross every single night in a strip club. There are all sorts of assumptions made about the character of strippers. The stigma of the title allows people to feel pretty clear about what kinds of things a stripper is willing to do in the club, out of the club, and especially sexually, period. The assumptions are oftentimes wrong.

Women are socialized to be nice and agreeable to the point of it being a detriment. I know many women who feel wrong causing friction even if they are in the right. These women don't want to be shunned from work opportunities. They don't want to get the reputation of being difficult to work with. They want to be understood. They want to be liked. They would rather avoid conflict than speak up for themselves. Some women will deal with being treated in ways that they do not desire in order to keep the peace. The only person that ends up feeling better about this is usually not the uncomfortable woman. Everyone else gets to feel "unbothered" about mistreating her. We don't have to suffer in silence. It is not good for us. Holding onto negative feelings will often manifest into physical ailments. It is physically not good for us.

As a dancer in the club, I needed to keep my energy and mood up. Therefore, if someone was talking to me in a way that I did not like, I could choose to walk away. I often did. But I was also at liberty to choose to calmly tell the customer how and why his behavior was not acceptable to me. I wouldn't scream or spew with anger. I wouldn't have a smile on my face though. I also wouldn't allow it to upset me. I learned to speak my truth clearly and go on with my night. I couldn't afford to let bad treatment sour my mood. One's mood is way too important in having a successful night at work. I had a customer once ask to touch me in a way that I wouldn't allow. He wanted a nipple in his mouth. I, in a matter of fact way, explained to him that if I allowed him to do what he was asking, it would stand to reason that I had let the customer before him do the same and the one before him and on and on. He clearly hadn't thought of it that way. Eye roll. He was only focused on what he thought he wanted in that moment. He went from being surprised that I wouldn't let him do what he wanted, to not wanting it at all. He agreed with me and we finished our time in VIP without any further issues.

I've had situations not work out as seamlessly. In those cases, I'd let security know that his time is up. I would not feel bad about the money he'd already spent. Payment is taken up front before the clock starts in the VIP room. I would not feel bad about a customer being angry at me, and I certainly I did not feel bad about causing "drama." In those scenarios, I was able to continue with my night feeling good about having stood up for myself. There is only feeling good to gain by making our boundaries clear.

When I first started, situations like this would make me squirm and feel super unsure of what to do. I'd second guess myself and the situation. Was I overreacting? There were times where advances that made me uncomfortable came from club management. Who wants to deal with that with their boss, no matter what the workplace is? It got easier and easier like everything else in life. It's like a muscle to build, constantly picking up the hefty weight of society programming you to go along to get along. Pick it up, curl it, then bring it to the ground repeatedly until the muscle has great power and sharp muscle memory. You'll wonder why you ever were afraid in the first place to honestly speak your truth.

I find in life that people very often keep what they dislike quiet and just hope it goes away. We have to remember that we teach people how to treat us. Therefore, in the same way that we should state our desires clearly, and make known what we do not like. It cuts down on the amount of unwanted experiences we manifest, creating a force field protection around you. Another benefit is that once you get it out, you can move on. It removes the need to play potential negative outcomes on repeat in our minds. Imagine having all that freed up mental space to think about ourselves, our goals, our own happiness. Imagine peace of mind.

In relationships, people will often not talk about very important things, like the desire to have children, money, lifestyle preferences, etc. We all have seen people get involved in relationships, marriages, have children in situations that they didn't really want. But they did it as one of those compromises of being in a relationship. It seldom leads to a healed relationship. It often leads to despair and resentment. The reward of being in more situations that bring you joy than not is a priceless benefit to pushing through those initial uncomfortable feelings. Making boundaries clear manifests enjoyable life experiences. It helps to fuel our inner peace.

What is the worst case scenario of you speaking your mind? People disagree with you. There's always a way to say something that is both clear and polite. Do you try to avoid conflict then resent not being treated the way you desire? Why do we expect people to intuit what we want? Not many people can read minds. How can we remember that it is better for everyone involved when we say clearly what is going on for us?

"Boundaries are a part of self-care. They are healthy, normal, and necessary." - **Doreen Virtue**

17) DO SOMETHING NICE
EXPECTING NOTHING IN
RETURN

"The true measure of a man is how he treats someone who can do him absolutely no good." - **Samuel Johnson**

The idea of doing something nice for the sake of an ego stroke or to get something in return is energetically the inverse of doing something nice just because... well, it's nice. I've only lived in big cities. I've experienced different circles of people. And the club is a microcosm of life. There were the dancers who would call other dancers in if they had a big spending customer. Often this customer had plenty of expendable income and would be willing to spend on whatever his favorite dancer asked him to. There were also the dancers who would go for blood if someone even blinked in the direction of "Their Regular Customer." It was not uncommon to hear conversations about how so and so stole x, y, and z's regular, as if club patrons were property. The energy surrounding these two different approaches could be felt in the energy vibrating off the person. In the presence of a dancer who freely shared the wealth, so to speak, there was a relaxed, easy vibe. The other type made people feel anxious in her presence. The relaxed dancer didn't feel as if she was doing it for any other reason than her unshaken confidence that she could always get more. She knew there always is more. Certainly, she would be the one that other dancers would return that type of favor to when possible. Reciprocity is our natural inclination as human beings. It goes without saying that the other dancer always worked alone and was never offered help.

In this age of reporting our comings and goings on social media, it's easy to get into the habit of sharing things consciously and subconsciously to get praise and "likes." It's a better feeling to always do nice things consistently with no one knowing anything about it. It feels really good to help another person when it is possible to do. The smallest acts of kindness can be the most positive moment in someone's day. Think about a time someone did something unexpectedly touching for you. How did it make you feel inside? Think about the kind things you've done for others. That feeling in your heart is battery power for your spirit. Our energy radiates from us. Whether we think people can read it or not, is of no consequence. Think about the people in your life whose very presence gives you a sense of calm. Think about the people who have an adverse effect. When the heart is filled with good, it manifests goodness.

Anything that helps us to diminish the importance of the ego is great work to be done. I also believe in adding to the energy we want to see more of in the world. Sometimes, when I need to attract money because funds are low, I will give away money. A few cents, a few dollars, whatever is the most I can do at the time. My life has benefited greatly by the generosity of others who are in a position to give. I want to be one of these people. Therefore, I do it now in the small ways in which I am able to. It is a gesture of gratitude to the Universe for always making sure I am taken care of. It is me empathizing with being in the position to receive versus being in the position to give. With knowing both sides of this, I am unable to turn a blind eye if I can spare it and the situations speaks to my heart. I live in New York City, where there are people asking for help at every turn. I can't possibly help everyone. But there is always a moment in the day when I can open a door, send an encouraging email, give someone an unexpected thank-you card, use my time to help or just a passing smile. The return on the investment with kindness for kindness sake is exponential.

Who can you send a thank you card? Who can you tell a kind story about an interaction with them? Who can you hold the door for? What small (or large) thing can you do for no other reason than it being a nice thing to do? Who can you send a small gift to brighten their day? Who can you make what you make for? In what ways can we make this a lifelong practice?

"Anonymously perform acts of kindness, expecting nothing in return, not even a thank-you. The universal all-creating Spirit responds to acts of kindness with the response: "How may I be kind to you?" - **Wayne Dyer**

18) THE POWER OF YOUR WHY

"He who has a why to live can bear almost any how." - **Nietzsche**

When I was younger, I decided that I never wanted to do work that I didn't want to do. The idea of going to the same place every single day never sounded like the way I wanted to live my life. There are plenty of people who take solace in steady predictability. A steady paycheck is nothing to turn one's nose up at, at all. Perhaps, for those people a steady paycheck and benefits means happiness. Not everyone that goes to an office every day feels tortured by it. Some may even quite enjoy it. I am not one of those people. The toll that kind of life takes on my spirit isn't worth any amount of money. Both living as an actor and life as a stripper got me quite accustomed to maneuvering the ups and downs of unpredictable income. There may be nights where you have a windfall of thousands of dollars and another night where you leave owing the club money for house fees and payouts to the DJ and other staff members.

What life exhibits to me over and over again, is that when I focus on showing up and taking action, everything works itself out. The road to the solutions showing up with synchronicity is to relax and continue to take action. The time between a solution being discovered or figured out is going to go by whether it's spent fretting or being faithful. In fact, the less fretful one's mind, the quicker that solution may show up. This is a challenge. When things are out of whack or has hit a bump is when we MOST need our mindset programmed to believe without a doubt that it's all being worked out. It seems many of us have a natural setting that goes to worry the minute something doesn't go smoothly or according to plan.

This is where a really strong 'why' is important. If you have no reason why you are burning to get up and get going every day, life is mundane. I perform because I have to perform. There have been periods in my life where I wasn't able to perform and I was sad every day. Life that consists of going to a place to do specified tasks, then go home, eat, sleep, maybe read or watch some TV, and do it all over again the next day, was like a torture chamber to me.

Stripping became the best way for me to support my desire to do acting work and have more freedom in my life. As a dancer and independent contractor, I had control over my time. If I did not want to go to work or needed to stay home to prepare for an audition, I could. The cons of the job were outweighed by the pros of having full control over how I set up my time. Performing means enough to me that I can deal with the uncertainty of a freelancer lifestyle.

Perhaps, your thing is stability. A great life to you means knowing what is coming in and when it is going to show up. That desire will make you feel great about getting up every day to go and do the work you have chosen to do. You know how many days you have off and how many days of vacation you get. You know that if you get sick, you have health insurance to cover you. All of this predictability makes your heart sing. And to live a life where there are many moments that our hearts sing is the point, isn't it?

Whether your why is to climb the corporate ladder or wanderlust yourself all over the world as a freelancer, your strong why will get you through every peak and valley of the journey.

What would be so worth it to you, that nothing could stop you from doing it? What is a goal that would make you super proud of yourself? What would you be doing whether you had a 9-5 or unemployed? What makes you excited to start a day?

*"When you walk in purpose, you collide with destiny." – **Ralph Buchanan***

19) INVEST IN YOURSELF

*"Invest in yourself first. Expect nothing from no one and be willing to work for everything." -***Tony Gaskins**

So many ideas, so little follow through to completion. This not only is the story of my life, it's the story of many. There are so many things that I want to learn, do, experience, and be. However, the only way they can be done is if I do them. How do we do that? I thought, initially, that I would keep a few things on the fire and whatever finished cooking first would be my next it. Nothing ever finished cooking. They were all on eternal simmer.

I like to use the example of professional athletes. These are people who are the best in the world at what they do for a living. Very few people on the planet get to do what they do for a living. These super humans need coaches to guide them in their game and championship winning journey. So, if the best athletes in the world need coaches, why wouldn't they be useful for us? The first time I heard of life coaching was from a strip club customer. I was telling him about the myriad of things I hoped to create. He replied, "Sounds like you could use a life coach." "What the heck is a life coach?" I asked. "Most of them will do one free session with you to see if you're a good fit to work with each other. I've used them in the past when I had specific business goals." Even though I had never heard of such a concept, I decided to try it anyway. I went online and searched for life coaches. I spoke to three. For me, the best part of it was having someone get the ideas that had been a jumble in my mind out and into a clear picture. The picture was clear, written out with measurable timelines for completion of actionable steps.

Accountability!

The idea of having weekly or bi-weekly calls with someone checking in to see where I was at with my goals was very appealing. I knew I'd more likely to get things done with someone checking in with me. Unlike most of the seminars I'd been to (and as a reformed seminar junkie, I've been to MANY), having a coach meant steps towards completion, not just a weekend long pep rally. Those pep rallies lead to good feelings but no concrete actions to take.The first coach I hired was because I had a block about being able to earn big money in one night as a stripper. I wasn't going home empty handed but I was not making the proverbial $1K per night. So, I hired a prosperity coach to help me. Yes I, a stripper, hired a coach who specialized in helping people get over their poverty consciousness and step into prosperity consciousness. Some people will say that I am good at asking for the pay that I want. What they don't know is how much I had to work on feeling confident and deserving enough to unflinchingly say my rates. There were many different exercises and rituals that my life coach had me integrate into my life. One was taking myself out to a very fancy dinner when I achieved an earning goal. Sounds very simple, right? For me, it wasn't. I still often get knots in my stomach whenever I am about to spend money on myself. It's one of those things that I have to have tools to work through in my life.

Creating new habits can sometimes be very challenging. I like to set myself up, so I can actually get things done. It started with having a coach help me with earning more at work. Coaches and mentors have helped to facilitate me travelling the world performing, live as a freelancer for over 20 years, reach performer goals, and to continue working on things that are a challenge to me in adulthood. Never be done learning.

I'm going to guess that I'm not the only one that is a superhero in some areas of life and still need much work on other parts of life. Growth can be uncomfortable and takes more discipline than we'd like to admit. What happens after doing uncomfortable things? What changes? After we experience growth and lessons from doing said things, we learn that the rewards are exponentially more worth it than hiding from the initial discomfort.

We generally are motivated to move away from pain, and avoiding discomfort and fear seems to make sense. We're just being proactive, right? As counterintuitive as it may feel in our minds, it is sometimes wrong. Challenge yourself to do something that scares you. Then, go a step further and hire someone to guide you through it. Stay with it through to completion. Keep a journal of the journey. Before writing this section, I flipped through journals and To-Do notebooks I had kept, to remind myself of what I once thought wasn't possible for me and was reminded of all of the things I actually completed. My journals reminded me of the power of writing goals down. Looking back, it makes me truly value the mentorship, consultants, and coaches who helped me check my completion boxes. When we complete things, it serves to increase and strengthen our self-confidence. Every time we say we are going to do something and don't, it shatters our confidence in ourselves bit by bit. Life manifests better results when we move through the world with the highest level of self-confidence possible.

Investing in myself is one of the best ways I've found to do that.

Have you ever tried to be self-taught at something? How consistent with it were you? Now think about the things you have had an instructor or mentor for. Was it easier to follow someone who's been there and done that? There are certain things we can learn easily on our own for whatever reason. I cannot honestly think of too many things that I have learned without someone teaching me how. At the very least, I watched those who I thought were great at what I wanted to learn. Who can you learn new habits from? Who can coach you past your blocks? Why not make the learning curve less steep if we can?

"Investing in yourself is the best investment you will ever make. It will not only improve your life, it will improve the lives of all those around you." - **Robin S. Sharma**

20) WHO'S THAT LADY?

"You must be the person you have never had the courage to be. Gradually, you will discover that you are that person, but until you can see this clearly, you must pretend and invent."

- Paulo Coelho

Everyone deserves to be their own superhero. Complete with theme music and costume. Cape not mandatory. I had to create a persona for work if I was going to make any money. Frankly, who I was as a person, was not the type of person who'd flirt with someone I found attractive, or worse, complete strangers that I did not find attractive and were potential customers. If I had to explain the feeling of jumping into my superhero persona, it would be likened to jumping off the edge of a cliff knowing I would fly, despite the fear in my belly. Once I jumped, I put myself into a space where walking up to strangers was easy. It's a headspace that I can turn on and off after years of practice. I'm more naturally inclined to stand awkwardly in a corner watching everything happen. Working the room just isn't my default setting. I'm perfectly happy to watch everything happening without being the center of attention.

However, the work persona I developed could do this without hesitation. That was the main key – no hesitating. Turn her on like a light switch. Click. If I hesitated at all, the thoughts and feelings that flowed through my introverted mind would start to percolate. And they'd keep percolating and gaining the strength of too strong coffee. My superhero was brave about initiating conversations with strangers. She had no problem being funny and engaging with customers. She was confident that customers would absolutely want to spend time with her.

- What are the areas in your life where you think, "If only I could be like *that*, my life would be better?"

- What are the things you would do?

- Where are the places you would go?

- What traits would you embrace?

Depending on your answers, you might be feeling overwhelmed with, "There's no way

I can be someone who does ALL of those things!" The good news is, you don't have to do all of them, all of the time... but then again, what if you could?

Who would that person be? What is that person like? How do they move? How do they greet strangers? How do they move through a room?

Ask yourself as many questions as you can about who your super persona is and how they get things done. This is your alter ego. It is your burlesque persona, superhero or whatever you want to call it. Tap into this hero whenever you need it and go fly. Allow the sound of your proverbial theme music to blare, drowning out the voices telling you what isn't true or useful. Most of us can't predict the future, yet the voices in our head often want to project our failure there. But really it doesn't matter whether we win or lose. The more we win (and even when we lose), we see that neither of those things kill us. Losing teaches invaluable lessons which make us better prepared for when we try again. Winning proves the voices in our head are just negatively over dramatic. When we face this reality, it becomes so much easier to navigate the realities of life. There is no reason for us to preemptively scare ourselves into thinking failure is the end.

I always knew that I needed my life to have freedom of movement at its core. I thought that would look like working on film and TV projects. But that hasn't happened yet and that's okay. Unfortunately, I wasted too much time mourning that my life wasn't the pretty picture I imagined as a teen. Things change, and often for the better. When I look at my life now, it still has freedom at its very core, which is most important to me. And this was accomplished by being flexible and going with the flow of the Universe as much as possible. Less and less bemoaning what should have been. More and more about appreciating what has manifested to be. Stripping and burlesque were never part of the plan. But both have greatly benefited my life and helped me cross things off my bucket list, like shoe shopping in Milan, which I joked around about for years. Burlesque is the reason that I was able to shoe shop in Milan.

I imagined my Milan shoe shopping trip would have been because I was wealthy or a celebrity or something. Instead, it was because I was the only Black performer accepted in the 2013 Milan Burlesque Awards, and I chose to crowd source so that I could afford to go. I talked to people that I knew who had had successful campaigns. I learned about all of the steps that I should take BEFORE even launching the campaign to improve my chances of success. My full-time job became that campaign. If people said remind me, I did (even if I had to remind them several times). I reached out to people one on one. I called people on the phone (and anyone who knows me knows that I am NOT a phone person). I reached my goal. I went to Milan for the first time. I laughed out loud when I remembered my joke and found myself shoe shopping in Milan. I took action. I said yes to these things I never would possibly have imagined for myself.

After several years of therapy, I think more now about the life I have. I think about it in terms of gratitude as often as possible. And even when I am in a downswing, I work my hardest to focus on the things I AM grateful for while continuing to take as much action as I can to change what I don't like. It makes a world of difference to the body and mind to think of the ways in which we are lucky, blessed, taken care of, and happy. If the voices in your head naturally veer towards the negative, call in your superhero. Let them fly you to the other side. Life will always have positives and negatives. The other alternative is death. So, wouldn't it make sense to make use of every tool at your disposal to reach your goals? What can you create with your imagination to help you get to to the you, you desire? Our imaginations are powerful. We've spent enough time using our imaginations to convince us why we should be scared to try. Powerful tool, our imaginations. What steps do you need to take to train yourself to imagine the inverse of what fear so forcefully convinces you to believe? We don't know what will happen. Fear is our imagination and we shouldn't be stopped by an imaginary friend. Why be stopped by our own imaginary fear?

"Simply take action. Do one small brave thing, and then next one will be easier, and soon confidence will flow. We know – fake it till you make it sounds catchier – but this actually works." - **Katty Kay**

21-Day Challenge

Week 4 (Day 16 - 20) This week we are going to actively seek out and pay attention to things that we are grateful for. Take notice of the abundance in your life as well. Write at least five five things you are grateful for and/or ways abundance showed up in your life this week. It could be finding a quarter or an unexpected windfall and anything in between.

Bonus: Save a dollar each day this week.

21-Day Challenge

Day 21 Now we dance! For two songs tonight or this morning (you can also choose to do this every night this week), dance to your favorite songs. Choose something that gets you feeling extra good. Dance at home alone, dance with your partner, go take a dance class or go out dancing at an event. But dance it out like no one is watching for two songs then write about how you feel post boogie session. Post video online with the hashtag #ZeroFZone!

Write to me about the 3 three of the most positive experiences you had while focusing in this way.

Bonus: Take the money that you saved and put it in an online savings account. Start saving for a sunny day!

CONCLUSION

There are times in life when I think self-help is a cruel joke that is meant to torment me as I go through challenges. However, I've learned that *that* thinking is off course. When I was younger, I imagined a life where everything was running smoothly all the time. In this life, I finally had it all figured out and things ran smoothly. That idea is, in fact, what creates the torment. After conversations with wealthy people, poor people, twenty-somethings, and fifty-somethings alike, there is a theme that runs through all experiences. Life comes with challenge after challenge after challenge. We may hear in the news about the big wins of the super wealthy or celebrities. What we aren't made aware of is that every super wealthy person has had to and continues to deal with failures and loses as well. The journey to many wins is lined with losses, mistakes, and incalculably valuable lessons. The highlight and focus is put on the wins. The losses are simply lessons we learn from in between the wins. The only way you don't get to the big wins is if you let the losses, challenges, mistakes, and fails stop you. Embrace them (remember when we were collecting No's way back in Chapter One?), they are the education that gets you to your goal. Be open to the idea that your wins may show up in ways you never would have imagined. They may look vastly different but they will be equally great if not better.

There are two types of people. Person One, will let the first failure stop them in their tracks. Person One sees failure as a sign to give up. It's really easy to think that mantras and having gratitude are easy and great when things are going well. Person Two tends to have more tenacity to try again despite failure. Person Two will look at the lessons learned from the failure. How do we move through life when things are not going well? What tools can we develop to keep us going through good times and, more importantly, bad times? The most important thing I did while working in clubs was to develop and strengthen my drive to keep going in the face of adversities and constant rejection. You know how we all hate rejection? As someone who has experienced rejection several times a week for about thirty years, I can tell you, rejection can't kill you. Initially, it feels bad but even that gets better. Everything in life is either a blessing or a lesson. Win-Win.

Look at life from angles that aren't natural for you. Think about things in several different ways. Explore why you've decided to put the judgement of good or bad into any experience. Some experiences are good and some scary bad. However, if you really think about it, *most* things are neutral. Life is a matter of choices and consequences. How will we choose to interpret the outcomes from our lives? What will we focus on as we go through our day? How will we treat the people we encounter? Will we choose to use our time coveting what someone else has accomplished or be too busy creating our own? Will our self-talk be as if we are our own best cheerleader? Will we be consistent?

Perfectionism is often an excuse for procrastination all dolled up. Perfectionism and lack of consistency are the thieves of many goals. How many more times will you say: "HEY, they took my idea!" Had you consistently worked on that idea a little at a time from the spark of it until someone else did your idea, where would you be in that journey by now? They may not even have shown up as a competitor. Even if they did, you'd be further along in your own journey with "it" than them. One of my uncles would often say, "Life ain't easy, but it ain't hard either."

I want to hear from you. Let's continue.

If you enjoyed this book, I would love to come talk to your group, class or conference to talk about the lessons of this book and/or lead a bespoke *S.T.R.I.P. Shift* workshop, keynote or class.I am the Self Actualization Strategist for survivors of sexual violence. If you are a woman who is also a survivor of sexual violence, I want to support you in curating the life you want guilt free.

Join the #ZeroFZone closed group if you are ready to discover how to shed the shame and second guessing of yourself to embrace your personal prowess so you can live YOUR OWN dream.

Want to work closer with me and dive even deeper? Fill out this application and schedule a decision making call with me. Whether in my small live online group program or working with me one on one I

will be available to support you every step
of the way.

45116150R00113

Made in the USA
Middletown, DE
13 May 2019